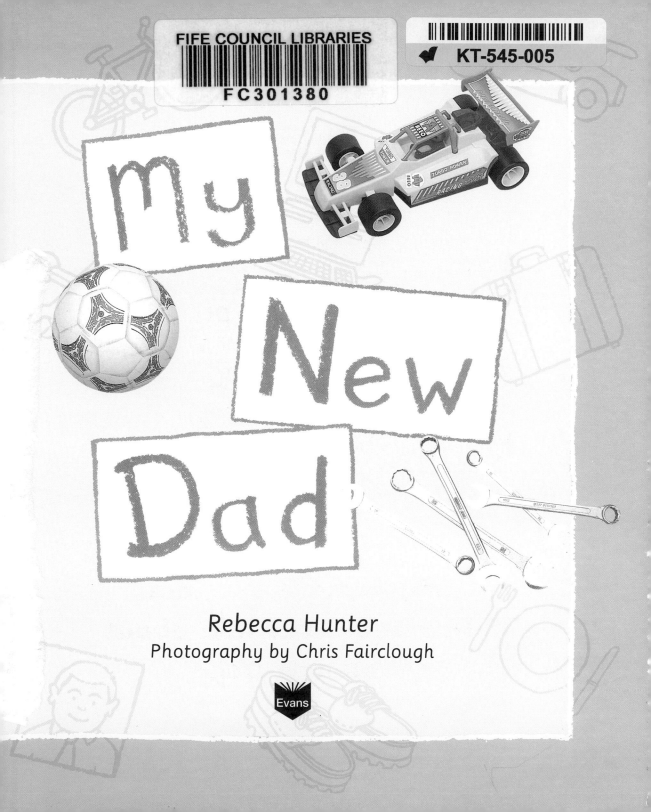

My New Dad

Rebecca Hunter

Photography by Chris Fairclough

Evans

First Times
My First Day at School
My First School Play
My New Sister
My First Visit to Hospital
My New Dad
Moving House
My First Pet
My First Visit to London

Published by Evans Brothers Ltd
2A Portman Mansions
Chiltern Street
London W1M 1LE
England

First published in 2000

Hunter, Rebecca
My new dad, - (First Times)
1. Stepfathers - Juvenile literature
1. Title
306.8'742

ISBN 0 237 52018 4

Acknowledgements
Planning and production by Discovery Books
Editor: Rebecca Hunter
Photographer: Chris Fairclough
Designer: Ian Winton
Consultant: Trevor Jellis M.A., M.Phil., A.F.B.Ps., Psychol. is a Chartered Psychologist who has spent thirty years working with individuals, schools, companies and major corporate institutions in the management of stress. He deals with individuals who are suffering from stress both in their family and in the workplace.

The publishers would like to thank William and Alice Allet and Mark Bower for their help in the preparation of this book.

Contents

Mum and Dad are divorced.

Mum and I live together in our house. Dad doesn't live here any more. Mum and Dad are divorced.

I stay with Dad at weekends.

I stay with Dad at weekends. I ask him if he will ever come home. He says this is his home now.

7

Mum has a boyfriend called Mark.

Mum has a boyfriend called Mark. Often they go out together. Sometimes he stays for dinner. He sits in Dad's chair.

Mum likes Mark.

Mum likes Mark a lot.
He makes her laugh.
He gives me presents
and tries to make me laugh.

Mark is coming to live with us.

Mark is coming to live with us.
He has brought two bicycles and
lots of bags and boxes.

Mark has too many things.

Mark has too many things.
We have to move our
things to make space.

I wish it was Dad moving in.

Mum cooks a special meal. I wish it was Dad moving in and not Mark. I don't feel like eating at all.

I am not happy.

Mum hugs Mark. They look very happy. No one asks if I am happy.

Mark makes me laugh.

We are
having a
picnic.

Mark plays football with me
and makes me laugh.

I feel bad.

I feel bad. I think my real Dad would be sad if he saw me having fun with Mark.

Dad says not to worry.

I go to see my real Dad. I tell him what is happening. Dad says not to worry. He loves me whatever happens.

Mark plays a game with me.

When I get home, Mark
and Mum are glad to see me.

Mark plays a game on the
computer with me.

I will have a new Dad.

Mark has
been living
with us for
a while now.
He and Mum
are going
to get married.

I will have a
new Dad.

18

I like my new Dad.

Mark and I are going for a bike ride.

I like my new Dad but I still love my real Dad best.

19

Index

Notes to Parents and Teachers

When a couple separate or divorce, a child will go through a period of mourning the loss of the parent who leaves while hoping their parents will get back together again. Although the child may eventually accept this situation, things could flare up again when a new partner moves in. This may be the time a child realises that the old parent has gone for good.

At first the child will resent having to share his/her natural parent's time with the step-parent and anger and jealousy will result. Once a step-parent has settled in, the child will inevitably compare the new with the old and one parent may come off worst. A child will often realise the manipulative potential in this situation and use it to cause trouble.

Children need to be prepared over a fairly long period for the changes that are to take place in their family environment. A new partner should attempt to get to know the child over several months, and spend several nights or weekends at the house before moving in for good. The couple should then keep public intimacy to a minimum for some time. Children should not be expected to call a step-parent Mummy or Daddy unless perhaps they have lost a parent through death, but the decision should really still be left to the child.

Estranged parents should try to concentrate on what is in the best interests of the child. It is important that they shouldn't criticise each other, and remain friendly in front of the child, although this needs to be done with care in case it gives the wrong signals to the child that they may be getting back together again.

• Both natural parents should emphasise to the child that despite the new arrangements, the child's place in their affections will not be changed.

• To begin with, the new partner should avoid being present when the natural parent collects or returns the child.

• Teachers should be informed as early as possible in the separation/divorce proceedings, so that they can be aware and allow for any change in behaviour of the child.

• Teachers can ensure that school provides a stable environment for a child whose home life may be unsettled.